The Aromatherapy Advocate

A Christian Handbook

The Aromatherapy Advocate

A Christian Handbook

By Naomi Ball
February 2013

Published By Naomi Eve Designs
Corvallis, Oregon

Thank you for purchasing The Aromatherapy Advocate, A Christian Handbook from Naomi Eve Aromatherapy.

The Aromatherapy Advocate, A Christian Handbook
Published: February 2013
Author: Naomi E Ball

For information about other products available from Naomi Eve Aromatherapy please visit www.aromatherapyforchristians.com or email at nball252@yahoo.com

 **About the Author**

Hi, I am Naomi Ball, a Christian, a certified aroma therapist and a work-at-home single mom. I home school my son and help my ailing parents. I was first introduced to essential oils about fifteen years ago and have been using them ever since. I enjoy studying about aromatherapy and I like to share what I have learned, without all the New Age philosophies that are so prevalent in most literature, on my website: www.aromatherapyforchristians.com.

Cover photograph by Rachel Patten.

My Oil Story

I was first introduced to essential oils by a lady with a toenail fungus. Gross, right? I had been a nail technician long enough to know that most over-the-counter nail fungus treatments don't work and the medicine prescribed by doctors can cause serious liver damage. When I gave this lady a pedicure I saw she had a toenail fungus and needed to see a doctor. She said she would use essential oils on it first. A month later she came back for another pedicure. That toenail fungus was almost gone, I was so surprised!! She said she had used Melaleuca alternifolia.

So I bought an essential oil kit and started using it for cuts and scrapes, bug bites, and sore muscles, but more importantly to help me sleep. First I tried lavender to help me sleep, after a moment or two I felt my whole body relax, I took a deep breath and went limp. However, it was a blend of essential oils that was calming and promoted sleep that helped me the most. I would put a drop or two in the palm of my hands and then lay down with my hands up to my face, which is how I sleep anyway. Every time it was a matter of minutes before I went to sleep!

The most profound experience I had with essential oils was on an emotional level. I was going through a really hard time in my life, without going into all that just know that it was bad. One day I was riding in the car feeling horrible, angry, bitter, resentful, hateful, etc. The emotions were a heavy oppression. Then I remembered I had in my purse an essential oil blend that was uplifting. I applied a drop or two like you would perfume. In just a minute or two that horrid oppressive feeling lifted and all those negative feelings floated away! So with a lot of praying, Bible reading, praise singing and anointing myself with essential oils I survived those awful times.

This is not the end of the story, just the beginning, I have been using essential oils ever since.

Table of Contents

SHORT HISTORY OF MEDICINE:

2000 B.C.—"Here, eat this root."
1000 A.D.—"That root is heathen, say this prayer."
1850 A.D.—"That prayer is superstition, drink this potion."
1940 A.D.—"That potion is snake oil, swallow this pill."
1985 A.D.—"That pill is ineffective, take this antibiotic."
2000 A.D.—"That antibiotic is artificial. Here, eat this root!"[1]

---

[1] Author unknown

Aromatherapy and Christianity

What is Aromatherapy?

Aromatherapy seems to be a popular marketing word that refers to anything that has a trace of flowers or has a drop of some plant extract in it. Words like organic, all natural, and green are hot words and advertisers know it. Unfortunately, however, all the marketing jargon, and even articles and books on the subject, have a lot of misinformation in them that lead to incorrect expectations when it comes to using aroma therapy simply because it is so popular.

True aromatherapy is the use of essential oils for emotional and physical healing. The English aromatherapist use essential oils diluted in massage oil and will tell you never to use essential oils without diluting them in carrier or vegetable oil. The French prefer to ingest essential oils and the German simply inhale. In America, true to American nature, we use the aroma therapy methods of many cultures for healing.

Should Christians Practice Aromatherapy?

This is something many people are concerned with. Some books and articles advise Christians against using all alternative medicine but especially aromatherapy because of the strong, fundamental connection to the occult and because it is not scientific. Most books lump together all forms of alternative medicine, however, just because channeling is New Age doesn't mean we should not use dried herbs. You have to look at each aspect individually to decide if it is a New Age practice or from some other Eastern religion or if it is simply biology, which was created by God. This kind of decision must be made with a good understanding of the background of each subject and with prayer and understanding of what the Bible says. Satan is very sly; he knows that if there is enough truth in his lies to sound good, people will believe the lie. There is just enough truth to alternative medicine that makes it all seem believable. There is some physical benefit to yoga, but it **is** a Hindu religious practice. There is enough electrical current in all living things to make "life energy" or "chi" seem plausible. It is a real concern but not something about which you would make an all-encompassing decision.

Most alternative practices treat the whole person, body, mind and soul. This is good, to a point: A person can only be truly well if his soul is well. The words spirit and soul are often used interchangeably and the definitions can be ambiguous. The best way to explain it is that the soul and/or spirit is the religiousness of our being, the part of us that needs God and can communicate with God. However, no drug, no herb, no amount of meditation can heal the soul, only God can! All healing comes from God, just as every breath we breathe is a gift from God, even if we use medicine, essential oils or herbs. Spiritual healing, despite what you read *everywhere*, can only come from God by way of Jesus. Only God's forgiveness and love can heal our sin sick souls, while aromatherapy can help heal the body and emotions.

Essential oils and herbs are used by New Age and Eastern religions but that doesn't make them evil. Using plants as medicine pre-dates any Eastern religion or New Age. In the beginning God created plants with healing benefits. He was the first aroma therapist and the first herbalist, and the first dietitian for that matter. He created the plants with healing properties, whether the plants are to eat, sniff or drink, therefore they are not evil.

Furthermore, to throw it all out just because it is not scientific is wrong too. There are so many variables involved, every body is different and will react differently to medicine. Every batch of herbal medicine or oil is slightly different (which will be explained later) and every persons attitude and spiritual health is different. Allopathic medicine (modern medicine) does not address a person's lifestyle, relationships, or spirituality. Just because there is no double blind, scientific clinical test to prove a hundred times over that lavender is healing for burns does not mean that lavender is no good. Even drugs and surgery don't work 100% of the time, and often have *serious* side effects. According to Dr. Mercola:

> 106,000 people die every year from adverse drug reactions
> 98,000 people die every year from medical error
> 37,000 people die every year from unnecessary procedures
> 32, 000 people die every year from surgery related complications[2]

Kurt Schnaubelt, Ph.D. in his book <u>Advanced Aromatherapy</u> said: "According to the American Association of Poison Control Centers, 809 cases of fatal poisonings and 6,407 cases of serious but nonfatal poisoning were reported caused by conventional pharmaceuticals between 1988 and 1989. In contrast, plant-based preparations caused 2 fatalities and 53 serious poisonings in the same time period. The most dangerous plants were not medicinal but were house plants or shrubs."[3] Deaths associated with use of dietary supplements or alternative medicines are rare, compared to the death toll from the medical errors and prescription drugs. Science doesn't have all the answers.

The point is to not <u>blindly</u> trust allopathic medicine or alternative medicine, carefully examine your options and prayerfully seek Gods direction. To say that only science can heal is limiting God, He can heal with or with out drugs, with or with out prayer, with or with out herbs and oils. God is bigger than science.

Buying From a New Age Store

Should Christians buy their essential oils from stores and/or people that are New Age, Buddhist, Wiccan or some other religion? The Apostle Paul addressed this exact issue in his first letter to the Church at Corinth, only the object of the discussion was meat, not essential oils. In those days the pagan temples would sell the meat in the local markets after it had been sacrificed. Some Christians at the time refused to eat it because it was unholy, but some Christians did not think it was unholy because they prayed over it. This is what Paul said:

---

[2] http://articles.mercola.com/sites/articles/archive/2003/11/26/death-by-medicine-part-one.aspx
[3] Schnaubelt, Kurt, Ph.D. <u>Advanced Aromatherapy</u>. Healing Arts Press. Rochester, Vermont. 1995 page 43

23 All things are lawful, but not all things are profitable. All things are lawful, but not all things edify. [24] Let no one seek his own *good*, but that of his neighbor. [25] Eat anything that is sold in the meat market without asking questions for conscience' sake; [26] FOR THE EARTH IS THE LORD'S, AND ALL IT CONTAINS. [27] If one of the unbelievers invites you and you want to go, eat anything that is set before you without asking questions for conscience' sake. [28] But if anyone says to you, "This is meat sacrificed to idols," do not eat *it*, for the sake of the one who informed *you*, and for conscience' sake; [29] I mean not your own conscience, but the other *man's*; for why is my freedom judged by another's conscience? [30] If I partake with thankfulness, why am I slandered concerning that for which I give thanks? [31] Whether, then, you eat or drink or whatever you do, do all to the glory of God. [32] Give no offense either to Jews or to Greeks or to the church of God; [33] just as I also please all men in all things, not seeking my own profit but the *profit* of the many, so that they may be saved.[4]

For myself, if a store or website is blatantly New Age or Wiccan I will pass by. After perusing the information, to determine if the quality is up to my standards, and I still don't see anything from any other religion, then I may buy from them. Often I will ask Gods blessings when I use essential oils, and when I receive new oils. I know that my house and my body belong to the Lord and His power is mightier that Satan's.

Aromatherapy and the Bible

The Bible does mention aromatherapy, or rather the use of aromatic plants, many times, 1035 times according to David Stewart[5]. The very first mention of aromatic plants is in Genesis chapter two as it describes where the Garden of Eden was. "The gold of that land is good; the bdellium and the onyx stone are there." Bdellium is the family of aromatic trees to which Frankincense and myrrh belong, both of which are often mentioned in the Bible.

The main purpose of the Bible is not to tell us about the daily lives of its characters but much more importantly, to show us how God reveled Himself to various people, and to us. However, we can learn a lot about the way people lived in those days, from the Bible and from other historic writings. They did use various plant oils for spiritual rituals and for healing and even for romantic encounters![6] The use of aromatic plants for oil and incense was common knowledge. In the book Songs of Solomon, he describes a locked garden with choice fruits, henna, nard plants, saffron, calamus, and cinnamon, trees of frankincense, myrrh, and aloes, along with all the finest spices[7]. The writers of the books of the Bible did not see the need to explain how to use aromatic oils; it was just customary.

---

[4] 1 Corinthians 10:23-33 (NAS)
[5] Stewart Ph.D., David. Healing Oils of the Bible, CARE Publication, Marble Hill, MO, page xix
[6] Through-out Song of Solomon
[7] Song of Solomon 4:12-15

In Exodus, as God was establishing the priesthood and all their duties, He gave a recipe for holy anointing oil and for holy incense that was to be made according to the work of a perfumer or apothecary. They already knew how to make anointing oil, this was a new recipe.

> " Moreover, the LORD spoke to Moses, saying, take also for yourself the finest of spices: of flowing myrrh five hundred shekels, and of fragrant cinnamon half as much, two hundred and fifty, and of fragrant cane two hundred and fifty, and of cassia five hundred, according to the shekel of the sanctuary, and of olive oil a hin. You shall make of these a holy anointing oil, a perfume mixture, the work of a perfumer; it shall be a holy anointing oil."[8]

This oil was used to anoint the tent of meetings and the furnishings in it, to consecrate them, "that they may be most holy: whatever touches them shall be holy"[9] However it was not to be used on anyone but the priests, nor should it be reproduced for other uses.[10]

Myrrh grows in Arabia and Eastern Africa. The bark of the myrrh tree is scored so that the resin drips out, which then hardens. It can be kept free flowing by adding a vegetable oil, like olive oil. Five hundred shekels is probably a little more than 15 ¼ pounds.[11] Cassia and cinnamon are both of the *Cinnamomum* family and were imported form India and Ceylon by the people of Ophir, along with other spices.[12]

Many scholars believe that fragrant cane is calamus also known as sweet flag. Deni Bown in his book Encyclopedia of Herbs says that the oil from sweet flag (Acorus calamus) is potentially toxic and has been banned in the US by the FDA.[13] It is found in the wild in North and East Asia. There is the possibility that the calamus mentioned in Exodus is not *Acorus calamus*, it could have been, according to Barnes Notes, lemongrass.[14] When you consider the fact that Exodus was written 1200 to 1400 years before Christ it is not surprising that we do not know exactly what fragrant can is.

---

[8] Exodus 30:22-25
[9] verse 29
[10] verses 32-33
[11] Barnes, Albert. Barnes' Notes on the Old and New Testaments, Volume Exodus-Ruth. Baker Book House, Grand Rapids, Michigan. 1980page 84
[12] Ibid.
[13] Bown, Deni. New Encyclopedia of Herbs and Their Uses. DK Publishing London. 2001 page 101
[14] Barnes, Albert. Barnes' Notes on the Old and New Testaments, Volume Exodus-Ruth. Baker Book House, Grand Rapids, Michigan. 1980. page 84

The Lord also gave Moses a recipe for incense[15] that was to be burned in the tabernacle every day in the morning and evening as a symbol of perpetual prayer. Once while they were in the desert a handful of men were stirring up rebellion against Moses. God told them to bring their censers with burning incense to the tabernacle so that He may indicate His favor. He did not choose the rebellious leaders, the ground opened up and they all fell in. But the grumbling against God still continued, so God caused a plague to destroy the people; but Moses and Aaron begged for their lives. God told Aaron to stop the plague by running among the tents with a censer of burning incense.[16]

Aromatic oils were used for less profound reasons too. For example both Isaiah 61:3 and Hebrews 1:9 mention using the oil of gladness and joy. Proverbs 27:9 says that oil can make the heart glad. Oils were used to fragrance garments[17], bed linen[18] and for perfume.[19] Pouches of frankincense and myrrh resin were worn on a string around the neck as perfume.[20]

Jesus spent a lot of his time on earth healing the sick; He cared deeply about their suffering. He preformed healing by laying his hands on people, and just by speaking. After a time of training his disciples Jesus sent them out on their own to preach, cast out demons and heal the sick. The disciples were given the gift of healing according to Matthew.[21] So the healings they preformed were miraculous, but they did use anointing oil according to Mark.[22]

In his letter to the Christians of the early church, James admonishes them to use anointing oils.

> "Is anyone among you sick? Then he must call for the elders of the church and they are to pray over him, anointing him with oil in the name of the Lord; 15 and the prayer offered in faith will restore the one who is sick, and the Lord will raise him up, and if he has committed sins, they will be forgiven him. 16 Therefore, confess your sins to one another, and pray for one another so that you may be healed, the effective prayer of a righteous man can accomplish much."[23]

To be healed you need to repent, confess to the church elders, pray with the church elders, and be anointed with oil. Repentance and receiving forgiveness can be very

---

[15] Exodus 30: 34-38
[16] Numbers 16:46-50
[17] Psalms 45:8
[18] Proverbs 7:15-17
[19] Song of Solomon 1:12, Exodus 30:25, Mark 14:3, and many others
[20] Song of Solomon 1:12-13
[21] Matthew 10:1
[22] Mark 6:7-13
[23] James 5:14-16

healing both physically and emotionally. Have you ever had the elders come pray with you? Just knowing that these wise and compassionate men cared enough to come and pray with you is very uplifting! God can heal you with or without all this but this process proves your contrite obedience.

Present Day

But what does that mean for us today?
"For we are the temple of the living God; just as God said 'I will dwell in them and walk among them and I will be their God and they shall be my people.'" 2 Corinthians 6:16

"Or do you not know that your body is a temple of the Holy Spirit who is in you, whom you have from God, and that you are not your own."
1 Corinthians 6:19

It is our responsibility as Christians to treat our bodies as a holy temple. Have you ever read in the Bible the detailed description of how the Tabernacle with its furniture and curtains were to be made? God wanted only the very best for His dwelling place. Good nutritious food and healing plants, which can be used in the form of essential oils are tools from God to help keep up our health. It is our duty to keep our bodies in the best possible condition and to use the tools that He put on this earth.

Aromatic Plants in the Bible

The following is a list of aromatic plants and oils mentioned in the Bible. (This list of aromatic plants mentioned in the Bible is from Healing Oils of the Bible by David Stewart. I used BibleGateway.com to look up the references.) Since the Bible was written so long ago and since the methods of plant classification were not established until the 1700's it is impossible to know for sure exactly what species the Bible is talking about. (References are according to New American Standard unless otherwise noted.)

Acacia	Aloes (sandalwood)	Calamus (King James)
Exodus 25:5	Numbers 24:6,	Exodus 30:23
Exodus 25:10	Psalm 45:8,	**Song of Solomon** 4:14
Exodus 25:13	Proverbs 7:17	Ezekiel 27:19
Exodus 25:23	**Song of Solomon** 4:14,	Cassia
Exodus 25:28	John 19:39	Exodus 30:24
Exodus 26:15	Anise	Psalm 45:8
Exodus 26:26	Matthew 23:23	Ezekiel 27:19
Exodus 26:32	(King James)	Cedarwood
Exodus 26:37	Balm or balsam	Leviticus 14:4
Exodus 27:1	Genesis 37:25	Leviticus 14:6
Exodus 27:6	Genesis 43:11	Leviticus 14:49
Exodus 30:1	Jeremiah 8:22	Leviticus 14:51
Exodus 30:5	Jeremiah 46:11	Leviticus 14:52
Exodus 35:7	Jeremiah 51:8	Numbers 19:6
Exodus 35:24	Ezekiel 27:17Bay	1 Kings 6:15
Exodus 36:20	Joshua 15:2	Ezra 3:7
Exodus 36:31	Joshua 15:5	Cinnamon
Exodus 36:36	Joshua 18:19	Exodus 30:23
Exodus 37:1	Acts 27:39	Proverbs 7:17
Exodus 37:10		**Song of Solomon** 4:14
Exodus 37:15		Revelation 18:13
Exodus 37:25	Bdellium	Fir
Exodus 37:28	Genesis 2:12	2 Samuel 6:5
Exodus 38:1	Numbers 11:7	Psalms 104:17
Exodus 38:6		Isaiah 44:14
Deuteronomy 10:3		Ezekiel 27:5
Isaiah 41:19		

Mint
   Matthew 23:23
   Luke 11:42
Mustard
   Matthew 13:31
   Matthew 17:20
   Mark 4:30
   Mark 4:31
   Luke 13:18
   Luke 13:19
   Luke 17:6

Myrrh
   Genesis 37:25
   Genesis 43:11
   Exodus 30:23
   Esther 2:12
   Psalm 45:8
   Proverbs 7:17
   Song of Sol.1:13
   Song of Sol. 3:6
   Song of Sol. 4:6
   Song of Sol. 4:14
   Song of Sol. 5:1
   Song of Sol. 5:5
   Song of Sol. 5:13
   Matthew 2:11
   Mark 15:23
   John 19:3

Myrtle
   Nehemiah 8:15
   Isaiah 41:19
   Isaiah 55:13
   Zechariah 1:8
   Zechariah 1:10
   Zechariah 1:11
Onycha
   Exodus 30:34
Pine
   Leviticus 26:16
   Isaiah 19:8
   Isaiah 33:9
   Jeremiah 15:9
   Lamentations 4:9
Rose of Sharon
   Song of Solomon 2:1
Rue
   Luke 11:42
Saffron
   Song of Solomon 4:14
Shittah (or acacia)
   Judges 7:22

Spikenard ("nard"
according to NAS)
   Song of Solomon 4:13
   Song of Solomon 4:14
   Mark 14:3
   John 12:3
Terebinth
   Isaiah 6:13
   Hosea 4:13
Wormwood
   Deuteronomy 29:18
   Proverbs 5:4
   Jeremiah 9:15
   Jeremiah 23:15
   Lamentations 3:15
   Lamentations 3:19
   Amos 5:7
   Amos 6:12
   Revelation 8:11

The Ancient and The-Not-So-Ancient

Other Ancient Cultures

Moses lived during the time when Egypt was at its greatest, at a time when mummification and fairly advance medicine was practiced. When he was living in the palace he was no doubt anointed with aromatic oil very often. Egyptians would soak plant material in goose fat, after a time they would remove the leaves or petals and replace them with new ones, until the goose fat was very aromatic. Then the fat would be formed into cones and placed on the heads of the rich and famous. As the heat of the day melted the goose fat it would run down into their hair and skin so they could smell it all day long. Perhaps Moses did this too.

Ancient Egyptian medicine was highly advanced for the time, (from around the 33rd century BC to the fall of the pharaohs) and included simple, non-invasive surgery, setting of bones and an extensive set of pharmacopoeia. While ancient Egyptian remedies are often characterized in modern culture by magical incantations and dubious ingredients, research in biomedical Egyptology shows they were often effective and sixty-seven percent of the known formulae complied with the 1973 British Pharmaceutical Codex. Medical texts stated specific steps of examination, diagnosis, prognosis and treatments that were often rational and appropriate.[24]

The great cultures of ancient times had a good understanding of healing plants. The *Shen Nong's Herbal Classic*, also called Shennong Emporer's Classic of Materia Medica, a 2000-year old Chinese medical book is considered the oldest book on oriental herbal medicine, and describes the use of 365 species of roots, grass, woods, furs, animals and stones. In ancient Greece at lest some of the Egyptian medical information was available to Hippocrates and some of the herbs or medicine were used by him and in his school. The ancient Romans used aromatic oils for bathing and for massage, they had elaborate bath houses, for man only, where they would rub oil on their skin then get in cold water, more oil, then a bath of tepid water, more oil and a bath of hot water. Women had to stay at home to bathe and do the best they could with all their pots of ointments and perfumes. There is a lot we have learned from these ancient cultures.

One of the earliest known methods for using aromatic or medicinal plants was "smoking" the leaves, like the American Indians still do, with bundles of burning leaves wafted around. In Nubia, in Africa, where water is scarce they would put smoking herbs

---

[24] http://en.wikipedia.org/wiki/Ancient_Egyptian_medicine

19

under the edge of their bed. Then they would sit on the edge of the bed and with the blanket make a tent around themselves and the smoking herbs.[25]

The medical texts of India, the "Ayurvedas", were written about the same time in history as the ancient Egyptian texts. Aromatic plants were used for perfume as well as for medicine and religious practices. Sandalwood, aloes, rose and jasmine were commonly used. Interestingly, it wasn't until the late tenth century that distillation was invented by an Arabian physician. This information spread to Europe and then to England with the Crusaders, so that by the 12th century marketing essential oils and perfume was big business.

However, because people did not know and understand how the infused oils, essential oils and the smoke brought about healing or altered moods, they attributed it to magic or supernatural powers. The oils and smoke were often used in religious ceremonies. People believed that sickness and disease was caused by evil spirits or demons and therefore needed the magic or supernatural to cause the evil to leave. With our vastly superior knowledge of science and understanding of how things work we view these beliefs as absolutely ludicrous. But perhaps it is not so far from the truth. Read the section about emotions.

New Age

"New Age" is not new. It incorporates Hinduism, Buddhism, Shamanism, Taoism, Paganism and Wicca. It became popular in the '60's with those that rejected tradition and materialism and in the '80's it became nationally acceptable. New Age is a mixture of many ancient metaphysical religions, you can choose "what ever works for you", and "anything goes", after all "it all leads to one place". However as Ravi Zacharias said "All religions are not the same. All religions do not point to God. All religions do not say that all religions are the same. At the heart of every religion is an uncompromising commitment to a particular way of defining who God is or is not and accordingly of defining life's purpose. Anyone who claims that all religions are the same betrays not only an ignorance of all religions but also a caricatured view of even the best-known ones. Every religion at its core is exclusive."[26]

New Age believers strive for utopia within, to be one with the universe and Mother Nature. But the main point or philosophy is that man can become one with god, and that every man can become deity. They believe that Jesus was a great spiritual leader, period. They reject that there is only one God and that Jesus it the only one way to God. New

[25] Tisserand, Robert B., The Art of Aromatherapy. Destiny Books, Rochester, Vermont 1977. page 105
[26] Zacharias, Ravi. Jesus Among Other Gods. W. Publishing Group, Nashville, Tennessee 2000

Age doctrine says that humans are currently estranged from god/universe due to a lack of insight concerning god's nature and reality. The Bible teaches that we are separated from God because of our sin and that only by believing in Jesus can we become His children.

New Age beliefs have become widely accepted and encouraged as something all good citizens of the earth should practice. It is widely taught in all self-help books, because New Age is basically a self-centered, humanistic religion, worshiping the created not the Creator. It is practiced in business and professional groups, social activists groups, ecological groups, feminist groups, etc. It is in mainstream marketing, books, magazines, TV, etc., especially for natural foods and products, holistic medicine, and anything that has to do with natural healthy living. Many New Age beliefs are so widely accepted that you may not know it is New Age.

One web site belonging to a wellness practitioner that uses essential oils said, "An astrological reading empowers you with the awareness to make wise choices and achieve life's goals. It validates your strength, illuminates your issues and shows you the path of greatest reward." At first glance that sound nice…but strangely familiar, isn't that what Satan said to Eve when she was in the Garden of Eden? Your eyes will be opened and you will be wise.[27] As Christians we should be seeking Gods direction, His strength and wisdom.[28] To rely on the stars, as the web site suggests, is plain and simple idolatry.

Beliefs of New Age include reincarnation, self powered inner transformation, extraterrestrials, chanting mantras, mediating on nothing, yoga, astrology, extrasensory perception, divination, shamanism (the belief that rocks, trees and animals have spirit beings), self-healing, your own reality, visualization and imagery (to make decisions and change your life) destiny, karma, creating your own truth, religious tolerance and moral diversity, global unity, god-consciousness, new consciousness, higher consciousness, astral projection (which is training your soul to leave your body and travel around), channeling spirits so they may speak through you or guide you, life energy, universal energy, aura, energy field, new world order, Age of Aquarius, Yin and Yang, chakra, etc.

Here is a list of some New Age practices associated with aromatherapy:

Pendulums are claimed to be powerful antenna that receives information from the vibrations and energy waves emitted by people, places, thoughts and things, a kind of electromagnetism. (This includes the practice of holding your wedding ring over your pregnant belly to see if you are having a boy or girl.) Some people say that the pendulum creates a bridge between the logical and intuitive parts of the mind and can help a person know what kind of essential oil their body needs.

Crystals- are used to "bless" oils or to help indicate which essential oil to use and to clean the inner self. They are claimed to give off energy that will heal, control dreams, and transmit information.

---

[27] Genesis 3
[28] Matthew 6:33

Charkas- according to ancient Hindu beliefs there are 7 energy centers in the body that correlate to levels of consciousness. Some aroma therapists believe that anointing these points on the body enhances the effectiveness of the oil.

Astrology- is a group of systems, traditions, and beliefs which hold that the relative positions of celestial bodies and related details can provide information about personality, human affairs and other "earthly" matters such as which essential oils to use and when. Aroma therapists that believe in astrology maintain that the planets rule the signs, the signs and charts rule a person's physical make-up, as well as what therapies the person needs, and that knowing which essential oil is recommended by the stars will augment and bring balance to that person's energy.

Music- The harmonies in New Age music are generally modal, consonant, or include a drone bass. The melodies are often repetitive, to create a hypnotic feeling, and sometimes recordings of nature sounds are used as an introduction to a track or throughout the piece. Pieces of up to thirty minutes are common. As a form of promoting relaxation, New Age music has evolved to include vocals, and has become more common, especially vocals featuring Native American, Sanskrit, or Tibetan influenced chants, or lyrics based on mythology such as Celtic legends or the realm of Faerie.

Vibration – all living things have a certain amount of electrical vibration, a fact of science. Essential oils have some vibration, some more than others. However it is created energy, it is not the Creator. New Agers believe this energy has religious significance, that it is all part of the universal god, and that they can manipulate the energy with their hands or thoughts.

Massage-Massage is good for circulation, sore muscles, over worked muscles, joint pain and more. Just keep in mind some of the theory behind it. According to Hindu and Chinese medicine there is energy that flows through the body along certain meridians. Massage therapists are taught this theory as fact and that they can manipulate the energy with their hands. So it is important that you find a massage therapist that doesn't believe in it.

The Bible says:

> **Leviticus 19:31** "Do not turn to mediums or spiritists; do not seek them out to be defiled by them. I am the LORD your God."

> **Deuteronomy 18:10-12** "There shall not be found among you anyone who makes his son or his daughter pass through the fire, one who uses divination, one who practices witchcraft, or one who interprets omens, or a sorcerer, or one who casts a spell, or a medium, or a spiritist, or one who calls up the dead. For whoever does these things is detestable to the LORD; and because of these detestable things the LORD your God will drive them out before you."

Healing the Spirit

Most of the literature you read about essential oils will claim that certain oils can heal the spirit as well as the body. When oil molecules are breathed in, the olfactory nerves sends signals to the emotional center of the brain. Certain oils will make you feel calmer; some will make you feel more joyful or glad. Since the emotions and the spirit are so closely related, who can say where one ends and the other begins, when a person feels more joyful or elevated they may believe that their spirit is affected. However, the spirit is a religious being, or the "religiousness" of our being, and can only be affected by a religious experience with Jesus. Only God can heal our spirit. When our emotions are lifted and negative feelings are removed we can be more responsive to God and His word, more sensitive to His presence, but that is not the same thing as healing the spirit. *Only God's forgiveness and His love can heal the spirit.*

Aromatherapy and Science

Invention of Drugs

From ancient times to fairly modern times plants were used effectively as medicine. By looking at history it would seem that the use of herbal medicine and essential oils was not effective because of so much sickness and early death. But it wasn't necessarily the medicine that was ineffective. There were many factors that inhibited general health and well being. The biggest factor was lack of sanitation, no indoor plumbing, sewage was open in the streets and there were many horses and other animals in the streets, adding to the muck. People did not bathe or wash often, nor was there refrigeration. Spices and strong herbs were used to disguise tainted food. There was also a general lack of information; books had to be hand copied and were therefore very expensive. Few people could even read. Most medicinal information was shared orally.

By the late eighteen hundreds aromatherapy moved from the medical industry to the food and perfume industries. Scientists learned how to identify and isolate individual chemicals in plants and were able to determine the most active ones. Because they were able to create drugs with one or two active ingredients they were able to patent their formulas and be the exclusive makers which meant they were able to make a lot of money. Plant oils soon lost their popularity as medicine and plant growers focused their efforts on perfume and food industries.

In the perfume and food industries the fragrance or flavor is what is important, not the purity or therapeutic quality. Additives were used to enhance the fragrance, and to create more volume. So over the years the general interest and common knowledge of the medicinal properties of essential oils was pushed aside. During this time more and more synthetic fragrances and flavors were used. However our bodies do not recognize these synthetic flavor and fragrance chemicals nor are the chemicals beneficial to our health, actually they cause more harm than good.

In the seventies the general public began to show more interest in natural medicines, including essential oils, but it wasn't until the nineties that the manufacturers got on the same bandwagon and began to produce more therapeutic grade essential oils. Part of the reason for this shift was the concern for over using antibiotics and a general lack of confidence in the use of so many pharmaceuticals. As more people became interested in essential oils they demanded therapeutic quality.

Scientific Evidence

There have been a lot of scientific studies done, however, the trouble comes from so many differences in the way the studies were done. Some studies were done with isolated chemical compounds. Some studies were done in Petri dishes, some with lab rats. Some were done with personal care products where the essential oil is so diluted it is barely there. Some were done with cheep, inferior essential oils. Some were done with synthetic oils. Some were done with copious amounts of essential oils. However there have been enough scientific studies done with quality therapeutic grade essential oils to show that essential oils are highly effective against infections and infectious diseases, very effective for use with emotions and are helpful for use with chronic degenerative conditions.

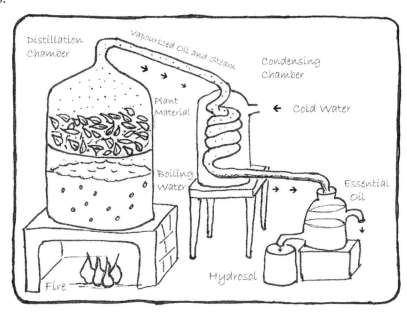

Terminology

The term aromatherapy is a widely used and missed used word. Now it is used to refer to anything that smells nice and may have a drop of essential oil or plant essence in it. However, originally the term was coined to refer to the use of essential oils for healing. Many products that claim to be aromatherapy have very little, if any plant essence in them.

Aromatherapy is therapy using essential oils. Essential oils are steam distilled from various plant materials. It is the concentrated plant essences. With one or two exceptions, all oils used for aromatherapy are steam distilled. Jasmine oil for example is an "absolute". **Absolutes** are made by using a chemical solvent to extract the fatty oils of the plant, such as jasmine. With jasmine steam distillation just doesn't work. Citrus oils are pressed from the rind without heat. It is the application of these oils that is aromatherapy.

Essential oils are steam distilled from various plant materials, or cold pressed.

Absolutes are oils that are extracted from various plant materials by using chemical solvents.

Fragrance oils are synthetic and have no healing properties.

CO2 Extracts are oils that are removed form the plant materiel with liquid CO_2, which is what we breathe out and plants use. If light pressure is used the extract is called "select" if more pressure is used and the oil is thick and waxy it is called "total". This is an excellent method of extraction because it is effective and leaves no residue in the essential oil.

Therapeutic Grade

Through out all history aromatic oils have been used for healing. However, with the advent of more sophisticated scientific medical methods interest in essential oils dropped off, so by the end of the nineteenth century to the middle of the twentieth there was little need for therapeutic grade oils. Therefore, manufacturers concentrated on fulfilling the needs of the perfume and flavoring industries. Manufacturers used methods to create more volume in less time with the only concern being to maintain the correct aroma. However, such methods destroy many of the complex and delicate constituents of the essential oil which make them affective as healing therapy.

Many variables affect the quality of essential oils, even the growing conditions, the amount of rain, the amount of sunlight, and the type of soil. So in order to create therapeutic grade oils it is necessary to use low pressure and low temperatures during distillation, and to use correct organic farming methods. Distillers, in order to create more volume, will use high temperatures and high pressure however. This destroys some of the more delicate chemical compounds in the oil. Also, they will distill the same plant material 2 and 3 times. Have you ever made 2 or 3 individual cups of tea with the same tea bag? The second and third cups are just not the same as the first. It is the same with distilling, the second and third batches are just not as potent as the first batch, but they can still market it as pure essential oil. Therefore, you will not get either the quality of essential oil, or the kind of results you are expecting from using essential oils.

Unscrupulous manufacturers will add synthetic chemicals to essential oils in order to create more volume. Here again you will not get the kind of results you are expecting and you may even get a skin reaction from the synthetic chemicals.

Uses of Aromatherapy

Aromatherapy can be used for a large variety of conditions. There are nearly 300 types of plants that are commonly distilled. Therapeutic grade essential oils are incredibly effective against infectious conditions and diseases, very effective for emotional conditions and are even helpful for chronic degenerative conditions.

Aromatherapy should not replace medical care. Aromatherapy can be used as a first step or in addition to medical treatment. Aromatherapy can be used to fight off cold and flue bugs, to treat minor cuts and scrapes, up-set stomachs, fungal infections, sore aching muscles, many skin conditions, etc., etc. If the condition doesn't improve, then by all means, see a medical professional. Also, using essential oils in addition to medical treatment can speed healing. Talk to your doctors or medical care provider about using essential oils with the treatments they recommend.

Anatomy of Smell

All smells are molecules that have been released from something. When you breathe, these molecules are drawn into your nose where they are detected by the olfactory nerves in the top of the nasal cavity; there are hundreds of millions of them. When you breathe deeply, increasing the turbulence of air in the nasal cavity, more odor molecules are carried up to the olfactory nerves. The bones surrounding the nasal cavity are called turbinates, they are designed to increase the turbulence in the nose enabling you to detect more smells.

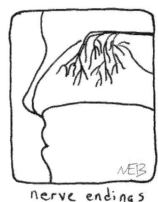
nerve endings

The mucus dissolves the odor molecules so that they may contact the olfactory nerve endings. The olfactory nerves are connected to the olfactory bulb in the brain. The information is carried by electrical impulse directly to the limbic system, the emotional center of the brain.[29] "The olfactory bulb transmits the impulse to the gustatory center (where the sensation of taste is perceived), the amygdala (where emotional memories are stored), and other parts of the limbic system of the brain."[30]

The sense of smell is the only one of the five senses that is directly connected to the emotional center of the brain. A particular scent can evoke memories instantly, sometimes even before we are aware of them. With the sense of smell we react first, then process the information. Information from the other sense are delivered to the thalamus, which acts as a switchboard and passes information to other parts of the brain.

"There are three basic functions of the limbic system: (1) emotional states and drives, (2) helping with memory storage and retrieval, and (3) linking the unconscious work of the brainstem with the conscious control of the cerebral cortex; the limbic system seems to be associated with pleasure and pain."[31] Because the limbic system is directly connected to those parts of the brain that control heart rate, blood pressure, breathing, memory, stress levels, and hormone balance, essential oils can have profound physiological and psychological effects. The limbic center can also activate the hypothalamus, which is the master hormone gland; it releases chemical messengers that can affect almost every function of the body. "Essential oils – through their fragrance

---

[29] Lazaroff, Michael J. Vieira, The Complete Idiot's Guide to Anatomy and Physiology, Penguin Group, 2004, page 339
[30] Essential Oil Desk Reference 3rd ed., Essential Science Publishing page12
[31] Lazaroff, Michael J. Vieira, The Complete Idiot's Guide to Anatomy and Physiology, Penguin Group, 2004, page 321

and unique molecular structure-can directly stimulate the limbic lobe and the hypothalamus. Not only can the inhalation of essential oils be used to combat stress and emotional trauma, but it can also stimulate the production of hormones from the hypothalamus."[32]

Chemistry of Essential Oils

A single essential oil is made up of several hundred chemicals. Scientists have been able to isolate some of these chemical compounds and have been able to understand how some of the chemicals can affect a person. Many of the chemicals can even be synthetically manufactured, and can even mimic the smell of certain essential oils. But because authentic essential oils are so complex there is no way they can be reproduced in a lab. Not only is essential oil chemistry complex but it can vary. The growing conditions, the condition of the soil, the amount of rain and sun can affect the chemical make up of the plant. The harvesting and processing can have a huge effect on the condition of the hundreds of chemicals in the oil, even the time of day the plant was harvested, the length of time from harvest to distillery, the amount of pressure and temperature in the distillery can all have dramatic affects.

Even though synthetic oils smell the same, they have very few of the chemical compounds that are in authentic essential oils, so there is no way they can have the same therapeutic affect on a person. Synthetic oils are chemically simple, and every batch made is just like the original, which is ideal for laboratory testing. However, every action of the mind or body is a vastly complex action of multiple chemical reaction and electrical impulses. Synthetic oils lack the subtle chemical compounds to balance out subtle conditions in the mind or body. The natural wholeness of authentic essential oils is more effective than any synthetic compound or even an isolated chemical.

Isolated chemicals can have potentially harmful effects, so when scientists do research on isolated chemicals of an oil they often warn that the essential oil is potentially harmful. However, God created these complicated plant oils with checks and balances, so the whole oil is safe and effective for many conditions. The other chemicals act as a buffer and balance them so they do not cause harm. Obviously some plants are just plain poisonous, but the 300 some oils that are used for aromatherapy are generally regarded as safe even if they contain a single isolated chemical which can be harmful.

Using essential oils will not make you numb to all emotions, like some drugs do, they will not make you forget, or have a foggy brain. Essential oils will help you feel like you can cope with the overwhelming emotions. They will make your emotions feel lighter and more elevated. Essential oils can help a person overcome some psychoneuroimmunological problems. (psycho-neuro-immune-ological) It is known that "aldehydes and esters of certain essential oils are very calming and sedating to the central nervous system (including both the sympathetic and parasympathetic systems). These

---

[32] Essential Oil Desk Reference 3rd ed., Essential Science Publishing page 12

substances allow us to relax instead of letting anxiety build up in our body."[33] So if you want to forget and be numb try something else.

The hard part is to know which oils to use for which condition, physical or emotional. Every person you ask or every book you look in, lists something different and the list may be rather long. So how do you know which oil to use? Kurt Schnaubelt Ph.D. maintains that classification system based on the chemical components of oils is the most logical and helpful way to decide which oil to use.[34] This system also helps in creating effective blends. Combining oils that have similar main components strengthens the effectiveness and are supported by the trace components.[35] His system is very helpful when it comes to physical symptoms. However, he lists only two chemical compounds as having any kind of emotional affect: Aldehydes are sedative and Phenylpropanes are stimulants. Melissa, citronella, eucalyptus citriodora and lemongrass are listed as having high aldehydes. Cinnamon and clove are the only ones he lists as having high Phenylpropane content.[36] This chart below may help you decide which oils to use.

Major Chemical Compounds	Most Common Action
Aldehydes	Sedative, anti-inflammatory, anti-viral
Ketones	Cell-regenerating, mucolytic, neurotoxic
Esters	Antispasmodic, equilibrating, antifungal
Phenylpropanes (Estragole, Anethole)	Antispasmodic, balances the autonomic nervous system
Phenylpropanes (Eugenol, Cinnamic Aldehyde)	Skin irritant, antibacterial, stimulant
Monoterpene Alcohols	Tonifying, antiseptic, antiviral, immune-stimulating
Phenols	Strong antibacterial, immune-stimulating, warming
Monoterpene Hydrocarbons	Antiviral, cortisone-like
Oxides	Expectorant [37]

Another thing to consider, which adds to the complexity, is that when essential oils are combined a new chemical formula is created, often enhancing the effectiveness of the individual oils. The human mind and body are so complicated and essential oils are also so complex, that it is nearly impossible to say *exactly* what affect an oil will have. Both the oil and the human are totally affected by the environment they each live in, and every body reacts differently, which adds to the complexity. So what do we have to go on when it comes to aromatherapy? We just have to trust the experiences of the experts, which by the way have thousands of years of experience!

---

[33] ibid, 237
[34] Schnaubelt, Kurt, Ph.D., Advanced Aromatherapy. Healing Arts Press, Rochester, Vermont, 1995. Page52.
[35] Ibid, 57
[36] ibid, page 55,
[37] Ibid, page 54

Emotions and Aromatherapy

A Merry Heart

> A merry heart does good, like medicine,
> But a broken spirit dries the bones.
>
> Proverbs 17:22 (NKJ)

Have you ever noticed how people are attracted to positive people and how good things seem to come their way? The opposite is also true, negative people tend to bring you down and negative things seem to always happen to them. Which are you? How can you make your life more positive and productive?

The first thing you have to understand is that your thoughts affect your life. How? Your back bone is connected to your hipbone. Your hipbone is connected…. all your body parts are connected to each other, including your brain, which is where thoughts happen. Your thoughts affect the way you feel, the way you feel affects the way you act and the way you act precipitates certain results. For example: years ago my cat woke me up 10 minutes before the alarm went off. I got mad and threw my pillow at him, which knocked over my favorite vase and broke it. I was mad at the cat so I got in a fight with my husband. Then I was running late for work. Then when I backed out of the drive way I didn't look both ways and backed into a parked car and broke the taillights! If I hadn't had been dwelling on my anger and all the wrong done to me I would have paid more attention to driving. My thought had affected my life.

Our thoughts are affected by how we perceive things. I believed the cat was just being ornery so I got mad. Which wasn't the case at all, he just had to go …outside. I was mad at the cat so I perceived that everything my husband said was wrong in some way. He reacted in kind. I tore out of the drive way in a huff perceiving the world was out to get me, and broke the tail lights. How different that whole day would have been if I had just gotten up with the cat and let him out, started the coffee and enjoyed a quiet moment!

The way you *perceive* any situation that comes up is going to affect your thoughts. The mood you are in, the troubles in your life that are spinning around in your head, your aches and pains, all these things will cloud your perception. If you are letting all these things put you in a bad mood you are going to see things in a negative light and *respond* in a negative way, which will have a negative affect on the situation.

Being in a bad mood is not our natural frame of mind; our natural state of mind is to be positive. When we are in a positive or good mood we see the world and the people around us as pleasant. We are more tolerant of negative people and situations, and we look for the good. We are more humorous and fun to be around, and we are more apt to be up-lifting to those around us. When we act positively and kindly to other people they will act positively to us and good things will come of it. That is our natural frame of mind.

Sin

Some people believe that the Bible is nothing more than a bunch of rules meant to take the fun out of living, but that is exactly the opposite. Jesus said, "I am come that you may have life and have it more abundantly" [38] God is perfect in all ways. He is all powerful, all knowing, in all places at one time and is absolutely good. He cannot abide in sin. Which leads to the worst result of sinning, it causes separation from God. The rules are meant to protect us.

In the beginning God created a beautiful, perfect garden[39] for a perfect Adam and a perfect Eve to live in. No one knows what was in that garden, or how big it was. It most likely had all kinds of fruit and vegetables for them to pick and eat. And herbs and aromatic plants! At that time God said they could eat any green plant that was good for food[40]. All animals lived in harmony with Adam and Eve. They didn't have to work for a living. God walked through the garden with them[41]. It was perfect and beautiful, it was how God intended people to live. But then….

When Adam and Eve sinned they were thrown out of the garden. They, the serpent that tempted them and the very ground was cursed by God. (Genesis chapter 3) Adam would have to work hard for food. The ground was cursed with thorns and thistles. And Eve was cursed with pain in childbirth. Because Adam and Eve sinned they were told they were going to die.

The worst thing they suffered was separation from God. God is the source of life, love and perfection. They could no longer walk with Him in the garden. They were cursed, rejected and thrown out, separated from God, how terrible they must have felt.

Later, in the Old Testament, God established a covenant with the Israelites, which did have a lot of rules and required an animal sacrifice in order to receive forgiveness. They had to make these sacrifices every year. But when Jesus died on the cross and rose from the dead He became our sacrifice once and for all.[42] In doing so He created a new covenant between God and us, a way for us to be completely forgiven and reunited with Him, healed spiritually. "For the law of the Spirit of life in Christ Jesus has set you free from the law of sin and of death. For what the Law could not do, weak as it was through the flesh, God did: sending His own Son in the likeness of sinful flesh and as an offering for sin,"[43] All the rules and animal sacrifices were summed up in one, the sacrifice of Jesus.

Sin is disobedience to the laws of God, which can only lead to negative and painful emotions. In his letter to the Church at Colossae the apostle Paul listed the following as

---

[38] John 10:10
[39] Genesis 2:8
[40] Genesis 1:29
[41] Genesis3:8
[42] Acts 10:43
[43] Romans 8:2-3

sin: immorality, impurity, passion, evil desire, greed[44] and anger, wrath, malice, slander, abusive speech, lying.[45] In his letter to the Galatians he lists immorality, impurity, sensuality, idolatry, sorcery, enmities, strife, jealousy, outbursts of anger, disputes, dissensions, factions, envying, drunkenness, carousing, and things like these.[46] A life of these kinds of actions would be a miserable, worsening spiral. It would be negative, painful, stressful life, leading to tension and anxiety.

Even though the Ten Commandments[47] are from the Old Testament they are still considered good rules to live by. The first four are about honoring God. The fifth one tells us to honor our parents and comes with a promise; if we do honor our parents we may enjoy a long life. The others are about murder, stealing, committing adultery, lying, and desiring what belongs to another. Most societies consider these good rules.

The little Sunday school object lesson really explains it well: imagine a branch with many smaller branches and twigs represents the law. If the branch is snapped off at the base, the widest part of the branch, then the branch is broken. If a tiny little twig is snapped off, then the branch is broken. Big branch or little twig, it is still broken. Big sin or little sin, God cannot over look it. It is quite evident that the sins listed above cause pain and heartache as well as in some cases physical pain and discomfort. "It [sin] leaves marks in our body and spirit, not just our soul. It creates suffering, illness, disease and, ultimately, an early death" [48] For us to live perfectly, with out sin is impossible, with out Gods help that is. God requires us to behave perfectly but He also provides help if we commit ourselves to Him.

When Jesus was asked which is the greatest law this is what He said, "Thou shalt love the Lord thy God with all thy heart, and with all thy soul, and with all thy mind. This is the great and first commandment. And a second like unto it is this; Thou shalt love thy neighbor as thyself. On these two commandments the whole law hangs, and the prophets."[49] He also said, "Therefore whatever you want others to do for you, do so for them, for this is the Law and the Prophets."[50] To live a life in obedience to God is quite simple, love God and love all people, and to practice love, joy, peace, patience, kindness, goodness, and faithfulness. The apostle Paul said, "Do nothing from selfishness or empty conceit, but with humility of mind let each of you regard one another as more important than him self; do not merely look out for your own personal interests, but also for the interests of others. Have this attitude in yourselves which was also in Christ Jesus,"[51] So when a person loves God and follows His rules then their life will be filled with "love, joy peace, patience, kindness, goodness, faithfulness, gentleness, self-control; against

---

[44] Colossians 3:5
[45] verses 8
[46] Galatians 5:19-21
[47] Exodus 20
[48] Lynn, Jim, The Miracle of Healing in Your Church Today, Trafford Publishing, Victoria, BC, Canada, 2002
[49] Matthew 22:37-40
[50] Matthew 7:12
[51] Philippians 2:3-5

such things there is no law."[52] In other words, living by the law of love is to live abundantly.

The Physical Effect of Negative Emotion

Atoms are made of electrical particles. Protons have a positive charge, electrons have a negative charge and neutrons are neutral. All cells have electrical energy, which can be measured as electromagnetic energy. [53] A scientific truth is that all things have electrical energy.

Buddhist, New Age and Hindu philosophies call the electrical energy of the body the life force, life energy or Chi. Is it the same as electromagnetic energy? The authors of Alternative Medicine the Christian Handbook do not believe it is the same. In comparing the two, "electromagnetic radiation can be detected in, and does emanate from, the human body. Many conventional diagnostic techniques make use of these effects, such as EEGs and EKGs. However, these are not what energy medicine means by its HEF [human electrical force]. Electromagnetic energies can be detected, generated, and studied objectively, while such studies have never been done with life energy."[54] The truth is our bodies do have electric energy but it is not the same thing as the life force that is connected to the universe, as some would believe. These philosophies of energy have warped and twisted the truth with the single purpose of leading people away from God the Creator.

All brain activity, including thought, is a complex chemical or electrical action, more complex than we can understand. Thoughts are transported by nerve cells to all the cells in our body, where they are imprinted on the DNA. [55] Anxiety, for example creates an acidic condition that is transcribed on to the RNA, which is then stored in the DNA. That emotion, the complex chemical and electrical action, then becomes a predominant factor in our lives.

> "Your body is in fact a very powerful electromagnetic transmitter and receiver of energy. Every thought you have can have a powerful impact on the cells in your body. Positive high vibration thoughts can rid your body of disease. Negative stressful low vibration thoughts can give your body disease. Science does not believe that thoughts can have any profound effect on your health. Medical science believes that thoughts could never alone cure or cause disease."[56]

---

[52] Galatians 5:22-23
[53] Lazaroff, Michael J. Vieira, The Complete Idiot's Guide to Anatomy and Physiology, Penguin Group, 2004, page 22
[54] O'Mathuna Ph.D., Donal, and Walt Larimore, M.D., Alternative Medicine the Christian Handbook, Zondervan Publishing House, Grand Rapids, Michigan. 2001. Page 196
[55] Truman, Karol K. Feelings Buried Alive Never Die, page 30. Olympus Publishing, Phoenix, Arizona 2003
[56] Trudeau, Kevin. Natural Cures "They" Don't Want You to Know About, page 109, Alliance Publishing Group, Inc, Elk Grove Village, Il

It is widely accepted fact that strong emotions such as fear, anger, hate, love and joy definitely impact your health. For example, the CEO who is under a lot of pressure and is always uptight and often angry has a heart attack, or the nervous and anxious co-ed has ulcers. When you feel stressed you are more apt to catch a cold.

The connection between emotions and health is not easily measurable; there are too many variables involved in a person's life to make double-blind studies effective. There is no machine that can measure how deeply a person feels anger, or how much anger is bottled up inside a person. There has been a lot written about this mind-body connection but a lot of it is rooted in Hindu and Buddhist philosophies. To accept other religious beliefs goes against what the Bible teaches.

However, there is a relatively new scientific/medical field of study called psychoneuroimmunology (phyco-neruo-immune-ology) that combines the study of psychology, neurology, immunology, endocrinology and several others. This field of study began more or less in 1975, doctors realized that the brain and mind are actually connected to the body. With this field of study they want to determine the mechanics of the brain/mind interaction with the body.

> "The main interests of PNI are the interactions between the nervous and immune systems and the relationships between mental processes and health. PNI studies, among other things, the physiological functioning of the neuroimmune system in health and disease;"[57] "The immune system and the brain talk to each other through signaling pathways. The brain and the immune system are the two major adaptive systems of the body. During an immune response the brain and the immune system "talk to each other" and this process is essential for maintaining homeostasis."[58] "There is now sufficient data to conclude that immune modulation by psychosocial stressors and/or interventions can lead to actual health changes. Although changes related to infectious disease and wound healing have provided the strongest evidence to date, the clinical importance of immunological disregulation is highlighted by increased risks across diverse conditions and diseases…. Stressors can produce profound health consequences. In one epidemiological study, for example, all-cause mortality increased in the month following a severe stressor – the death of a spouse. Theorists propose that stressful events trigger cognitive and affective responses which, in turn, induce sympathetic nervous system and endocrine changes, and these ultimately impair immune function. Potential health consequences are broad, but include rates of infection HIV progression and cancer incidence and progression.
>
> Stress is thought to affect immune function through emotional and/or behavioral manifestations such as anxiety, fear, tension, anger and sadness

---

[57] http://en.wikipedia.org/wiki/Psychoneuroimmunology
[58] ibid.

and physiological changes such as heart rate, blood pressure, and sweating. Researchers have suggested that these changes are beneficial if they are of limited duration, but when stress is chronic, the system is unable to maintain equilibrium or homeostasis."[59]

So, yes there is scientific evidence as well as common sense that negative and positive emotions play a large role in our health. Positive thoughts and emotions build us up, strengthening our immune systems, as well as all systems, and negative thoughts and feelings tear us down. The amazing thing is that our feelings are contagious. The way we feel affects the way we perceive things in our lives; the way we perceive things affects the way we react. The way we react affects other people's feelings and the way they react to us affects the way we feel. When this cycle is going negatively you can change it, by realizing that you are reacting in a negative way because of the way you are feeling, and you can make up your mind to react positively which will then lead you to feel positive.

Karol K. Truman in her book <u>Feelings Buried Alive Never Die</u> has an extensive list of diseases and the probable emotions that caused them. For example: abscesses could possible be caused by any of the following; seething, unresolved hurt feelings, wanting revenge, festering feelings, stagnation or holding on to an old concept. Diabetes could be caused by judging self or others severely, disappointment in life, on-going feelings of sorrow, emotional shock, joy of life is gone, feeling "it should have been different", obsessed with wanting control or ashamed of something you did in the past. Eczema could be caused by being over-sensitive, feeling you are being interfered with or prevented from doing something, thus feeling frustrated, unresolved hurt feelings or unresolved feelings of irritation.[60] This certainly isn't a scientifically proven list but it could be used as a tool, a step in the right direction towards healing.

The Role of Forgiveness

Healing cannot begin unless there is forgiveness.[61] When we are repentant, ready to stop doing what we were doing and we ask God to forgive us for the sin we have done He will forgive and forget that sin.

    "As far as the east is from the west,
    So far has He removed our transgressions from us."
    Psalms 103:12

Every time! He will cleanse our hearts and heal our spirits. "Confession purges the soul of evil, much like a stomach regurgitates bad food. It is a cleansing action needed for the body, spirit, and soul to be healthy. Once confessed, a flood of relief and peace is often

---

[59] ibid.

[60] Truman, Karol K. <u>Feelings Buried Alive Never Die</u>, Olympus Distributing, Phoenix, Arizona, 1991 page 225-271

[61] James 5:16

35

experienced, a healing in itself."[62] With the feeling of peace and release, and the power of God we can begin to heal emotionally. "Now may the God of **peace** Himself sanctify you entirely; and may your spirit and soul and body be preserved complete, without blame at the coming of our Lord Jesus Christ." 1 Thessalonians 5:23. When we forgive others or ourselves for whatever reason, we experience the same peace and release of negative pent-up feelings. "For if you **forgive** others for their transgressions, your heavenly Father will also **forgive** you." Matthew 6:14. Our bodies were designed to be reliant on the Creator; he wants our total devotion and adoration. Over and over the Bible says if we follow His laws we will receive His blessings and healing. He created our bodies to have the emotional connection, to be affected by our emotions and to have that dependence on His forgiveness.

Praise and Worship

God loves you. He wants to heal you. One of the best ways to overcome negative emotions is to praise God. When you are feeling hateful and mean or depressed and miserable the last thing you <u>feel</u> like doing is singing praise songs, but that is the best thing to do. If you can't bring yourself to sing then read Psalms. When I was going through a hard time in my life I would search Psalms for the most praiseful ones and read them over and over. I didn't have the capacity to praise God with my own words, but God knew my heart and used David's words to lift me above my misery. When you are in the middle of a really rough time you don't feel like reading the Bible, praying, and praising God, so you should make up your mind to <u>do it anyway</u>. Tell God how you feel and ask Him to help. He will. He loves you.

---

[62] Lynn, Jim. <u>The Miracle of Healing in Your Church Today</u>. Trafford Publishing, 2002 page 189

How to Use Essential Oils safely

Therapeutic grade essential oils are relatively safe to use if you follow a few common safety rules. Cheap or synthetically altered oils can cause a rash or some other side affects. The most common affect is skin reaction, a stinging burning sensation or a rash. People with plant allergies may have allergic reactions.

Keep in mind that essential oils are very concentrated, all you will ever use is a couple drops at a time. One little ten or fifteen milliliter bottle of essential oil should last for quite a while.

Skin Safety

- Do a skin test before using a new essential oil. Simply add a drop of oil to the inside of your elbow and wait at least 24 hours to see if you have any kind of reaction.
- Do not get essential oils in your eyes, nose, ears or other sensitive, private areas.
- If your skin reacts with a stinging burning sensation or a rash, rub in olive or other vegetable oil. <u>Do not try to wash off the oil with water</u>, water will cause it to spread even more.
- If applying oils directly on your skin mix it with olive or other vegetable oil, at least until you are familiar with the oil and know that you will not have a reaction.
- Some oils like clove, cinnamon, oregano and cassia should never be put on the skin unless diluted with a vegetable oil.
- Citrus oils cause sensitivity to the sun. Wait a couple hours after applying it to your skin before you spend any time outside.
- Add essential oils to your bath gel **before** adding it to the bath water. This will disperse the oil throughout the water; otherwise the oil will float on top of the water and may cause skin irritation.
- Don't use essential oils on babies or very small children, oils may be used in a diffuser or spray bottle if used sparingly; but not directly on the little ones.

Storage

- Keep oils out of reach of small children.
- Store bottles of essential oils <u>out of direct sunlight</u> and away from electrical equipment.
- Keep lids tightly closed, essential oils evaporate easily.
- <u>Do not touch the orifice reducer</u> (the plastic thing in the neck of the bottle); it is designed to funnel the last drop back into the bottle. If you touch it then the dirt and oils from your skin will go into the bottle and cause it to go bad.
- Store all essential oils and carrier oils in brown bottles.
- Keep oils away from open flames, essential oils are potentially flammable.

Precautions

- It is recommended that pregnant women should seek expert advice from a health care professional before using essential oils.
- It is recommended that people with epilepsy or high blood pressure consult a health care professional before using essential oils. Use with caution or avoid hyssop, fennel, basil, birch, nutmeg, rosemary, peppermint, sage, tarragon and Idaho tansy.
- Some oils should not be used on small children but for the most part use half as much essential oil diluted in olive or other vegetable oil. The essential oils listed in the ingredients in this book are "generally regarded as safe" except cinnamon. In this book cinnamon is only recommended for lip balm.
- Don't use essential oils on babies or very small children, oils may be used in a diffuser or spray bottle to spray into the air, but not directly on the little ones.
- Do not take internally, except for rubbing a drop on your gums for a tooth ache.

Different Ways to Use Essential Oils

- To use, hold the bottle in your right hand and allow a drop or two to fall into the palm of your left hand. Then rub your palms together, then rub onto location,
- Or you can mix essential oils with a vegetable oil, such as olive, in a large spoon or small bowel, if you need just a few drops.
- Use a cold air diffuser or nebulizer. Don't use one that heats the oil.
- Fill a mister bottle with distilled water and add your favorite essential oil. Shake the bottle well before spraying it around the room. This is a good way to calm small children. (Spray around the room not on the baby!)
- Add several drops of oil to a cotton ball and stick it in the air vents in the car or house. Don't use oils in the car that tend to make you sleepy!
- If you have done a skin test you can apply essential oil in grape seed oil like you would perfume, on your neck and behind your ears.
- Add essential oils to fragrance free massage oil or lotion.
- Apply essential oils to the soles of your feet.
- Add to bath salts. Fill a jar with Epsom salts, add several drops of your oil, put the lid on tight and shake the jar to mix it. Then let it sit for a day or two.
- Fold a piece of paper or card stock in accordion pleats, tape one end together and spread out the other so you have a fan. Then add a drop or two of essential oil and fan yourself. (Some essential oils will leave a residue and if your blend has a vegetable oil in it then it will leave a grease mark, so you don't want to use it on a fancy fan.)
- Add essential oils to your bath gel. This will disperse the oil throughout the water, otherwise the oil will float on top of the water and may cause skin irritation.
- Put a few drops of oil in a bowl of hot water, lean over it and cover your head and the bowl with a towel. This is good for a facial, or for colds.
- To help with fevers, put cold water in a bowl, add a couple drops of peppermint, stir it up and while the water is still swirling drop in the wash cloth then wring it out and apply to the person's forehead. This is a type of compress. This method can be used for any hot or cold compress, with the appropriate oils.

Essential Oil Profiles

Not all of the oils profiled here are in the Bible; these have been chosen because of their versatility, and reasonable price. (Rose oil *is* lovely but it costs two dollars a drop!)

Common Name of Oil: Bergamot

Family: Rutaceae Genus

Genus and Species: *Citris bergamia*

Countries of Origin: Asia and Italy

General Description of Plant: Delicate citrus tree with small round fruits.

Main Chemical Components: terpene hydrocarbons

Parts used: cold pressed from the rind

History and Biblical Reference: used to flavor Earl Gray tea

Key Use: recommended for oily skin, acne, abbesses, rub on the belly for indigestion, good for many skin problems, and cold sores

Emotional Uses: recommended for anxiety, depression, it is calming and soothing

Additional Notes: Don't confuse this bergamot with an annual herb by the same name.

Common Name of Oil: Cedarwood

Family: Pinaceae

Genus and Species: *Cedrus atlantica* or *Juniper virginina*

Countries of Origin: Morocco and Algeria, *Juniper virginina* from USA

General Description of Plant: a tall evergreen with needles

Parts Used: wood

Main Chemical Components: sesquiterpenes and sesquiterpenols

History and Biblical Reference: Cedarwood is often mentioned in the Bible as Cedar of Lebanon. King David used a lot of it to build his palace. Cedarwood is used in ritual cleansing, see Leviticus 14: 3-6 and 49-52. The Egyptians used Cedarwood in the embalming process and as a perfume ingredient.

Key Use: Helps improve mental clarity, helps control oily skin, recommended for acne, cellulite, dandruff, dry skin, (in other words it balances the amount of oil your skin secretes) insect repellent, fungal infections.

Emotional Uses: for anxiety and nervous tension

Common Name of Oil: Chamomile, German

Family: Asteraceae

Genus, and Species: *Matricaria recuttita*

Countries of Origin: Eastern Europe

General Description of Plant: a plant with daisy-like flowers that smell like apples

Parts Used: flowers

Main Chemical Components: sesquiterpenes, -a bisabolol, chamazulene

History and Biblical Reference: German Chamomile (Matricaria recuttita) tea was made famous by Peter Rabbit.

Key Use: calming, recommended for skin problems, anti-inflammatory, for insomnia, soothes stomach aches and indigestion

Emotional Uses: for nervousness and hyperactive children

Safety Data: may irritate the skin

Common Name of Oil: Cinnamon

Family: Lauraceae

Genus and Species: *Cinnamomum zeylancium*

Countries of Origin: Sri Lanka, India, Madagascar

General Description of Plant: tall evergreen tree with small white flowers and bluish fruit when fully ripe

Parts Used: mostly inner dried bark and also the leaves which makes a more gentle oil

Main Chemical Components: cinnamaldehyde

History and Biblical Reference: Part of the Holy Anointing oil as described in Exodus 30, also named in Proverbs 1:17, Song of Solomon 4:14 and Revelation 18;13[63]

Key Use: antibacterial, antiviral and antifungal, use for tooth aches, mouth care, use in a diffuser for respiratory problems (coughs, colds and flu)

Safety Data: Can be very toxic and much care must be taken when using it. It is a skin irritant and can cause a burning sensation and redness. Do not use in bath water and do not use while pregnant

Common Name of Oil: Citronella

Family: Poaceae

Genus and Species: *Cymbopogon nardus*

Countries of Origin: India, Sri Lanka

General Description of Plant: tall grass

Parts Used: leaves

Main Chemical Components: terpene alcohols

Key Use: antibacterial, antifungal, bug repellent, recommended for menstrual discomfort, bug bites, acne, headaches, and exhaustion

Emotional Uses: uplifting

Safety Data: May cause skin irritation

Common Name of Oil: Eucalyptus

Family: Myrtaceae

Genus: *Eucalyptus*

Species: *globulus, radiata, australiana, ordives, or citriodora,*

Countries of Origin: Australia (75% of all flora), Brazil, France

General Description of Plant: tall evergreen tree

---

[63] Stewart, David Ph. D. Healing Oils of the Bible, CARE Publishing 2002, Marble Hill MO. page 286

Parts Used: Leaves and small twigs, harvested twice a year, one well-cultivated tree can produce 100 pounds of leaves a year

Main Chemical Components: E. globulus: terpene hydrocarbons, E. radiata: terpene alcohols

History and Biblical Reference: E. globulus was discovered in 1792 in Tasmania.

Key Use: E. globulus is used for colds, coughs, most respiratory conditions, insect bites, concentration, muscular aches and pains, sore throat, skin infections, skin ulcers, and slow circulation.

Additional Notes: There are several forms of each type of Eucalyptus and some can "morph" into another form.

Common Name of Oil: Frankincense

Family: Burseraceae

Genus and Species: *Boswellia caterii*

Countries of Origin: Oman, Somalia, Ethiopia, Saudi Arabia

General Description of Plant: thorny shrub

Parts Used: resin, the bark is cut, the resin seeps out and turns to hard chunks

Main Chemical Components: Monoterpene hydrocarbon

History and Biblical Reference: Used in the Holy Anointing Oil and Incense in the Old Testament which were used in worship and cleansing rituals, see Exodus chapter 30, see Numbers 16:47-50, Aaron saves the people from a plague with the incense.

The wise men gave it to Jesus when the visited him as a baby. Most people believe that it was given to help finance their trip to Egypt but it is possible that Mary kept it and used it for healing and protecting Jesus' health while he was growing up. It was so commonly used that the words incense and frankincense are used interchangeably in the Bible. The Egyptians used it to treat everything from head to toe.

Key Use: everything, for skin problems, circulation, colds and coughs, for infections, a general tonic, antibacterial.

Emotional Uses: for nervousness and depression

Common Name of Oil: Lavender

Family: Lamiaceae

Genus and Species: *Lavandula angustifolia*

Countries of Origin: France, USA, Ukraine, Bulgaria

General Description of Plant: short bushy plant with spike-shaped leaves and purple flowers tightly packed around a single stem

Parts Used: flowering tops

Main Chemical Components: linalol, linalyl acetate

History and Biblical Reference: The Romans and Greeks used it in their baths and it has been cultivated ever since.

Key Use: every skin problem, insomnia, muscle relaxer, excellent for burns, acne, cuts and scrapes especially if infected, bug bites, sunburn (put in a mister bottle with distilled water to spray on sunburns), headaches, to balance oiliness of skin

Emotional Uses: for nervous tension, depression, to relax, calming

Safety Data: safe to use directly on your skin, safe for children

Additional Notes: The name "lavender" is derived from the Latin lavare, meaning, "to wash'

Common Name of Oil: Lemon

Family: Rutaceae

Genus and Species: *Citrus limon*

Countries of Origin: USA, Italy, Asia

General Description of Plant: tree, shiny oval leaves

Parts Used: cold pressed from the rind

Main Chemical Components: limonene

History and Biblical Reference: Native to China, introduced to Middle East in 1100s, Columbus brought to the Americas.

Key Use: antiseptic, antibacterial, stimulates digestion, anti-bacterial

Emotional Uses: uplifting and calming, for anxiety, promotes feelings of well being

Safety Data: Causes sun sensitivity. Wait 8 hours after using it on your skin to go outside, may cause skin irritation.

Additional Notes: Use to rinse fruit and vegetables: add a few drops to a large bowl of water to rinse produce. Use as an air purifier. It is recommended for dull oily skin, and repels bugs.

Common Name of Oil: Orange, Sweet

Family: Rutaceae

Genus and Species: *Critus sinensis*

Countries of Origin: USA, China, Africa, Italy

General Description of Plant: evergreen tree, dark leathery leaves, delicately perfumed flowers

Parts Used: cold pressed from the rind

Main Chemical Components: limonene

Key Use: calming, anti-inflammatory, improves circulation, helps insomnia, an appetite stimulant, good for dull, oily skin

Emotional Uses: calming, up-lifting, helps with depression

Safety Data: may cause sun sensitivity, stay out of the sun for several hours after using on the skin, may cause skin irritation

Common Name of Oil: Peppermint

Family: Lamiaceae

Genus and Species: *Mentha piperita*

Countries of Origin: USA, England, France, Russia, China

General Description of Plant: dark green perennial growing about 2 feet high, with underground runners

Parts Used: leaves and stems, just before flowering

Main Chemical Components: menthol, menthone

History and Biblical Reference: Mentioned in the Bible as part of tithing, see Matthew 23:23, and Luke 11:42.

Key Use: muscle relaxer, for sinus trouble (runny or stuffed), fever reducer, anti-inflammatory, cooling, for indigestion and gas, headaches, bug bites, rashes, use as an air freshener, for concentration, is stimulating, use for fatigue

Emotional Uses: uplifting, mentally clarifying

Safety Data: can feel "hot", do not use close to your eyes or in your ears, do not add to bath water

Common Name of Oil: Rosemary

Family: Lamiaceae

Genus and Species: *Rosmarinus officialis*

Countries of Origin: Mediterranean

General Description of Plant: shrubby evergreen with stiff needle-like leaves and blue or white flowers

Parts Used: leaves

Main Chemical Components: depends on the type

History and Biblical Reference: Used during Biblical times but not mentioned in the Bible.

Folk lore: the plant originally had white flowers until the Virgin Mary laid her cloak on a bush which caused the flowers to change color.

Key Use: recommended for skin care and hair loss, good for "wake-up" blends, chest conditions, and tight muscles and it is anti-fungal

Emotional Uses: emotional exhaustion- it clears the head, recommended for depression and apathy

Safety Data: avoid if epileptic, pregnant or have high blood pressure

Common Name of Oil: Tea Tree

Family: Myrtacea

Genus and Species: *Melaleuca alternifolia*

Countries of Origin: Australia

General Description of Plant: small tree or shrub with narrow leaves and papery bark

Parts Used: leaves

Main Chemical Components: terpene alcohols

Key Use: fungal infections, immune stimulating, skin conditions, dandruff, anti-bacterial, recommended for toenail infections and athlete's foot, for cuts, scrapes and bug bites

Safety Data: Safe for children and dogs but over use can result in sensitization, it is nonirritating. For children always use half as much essential oil as is recommended. Use only one drop on dogs or cats.

Recipes

Most of these recipes should be done in the kitchen where you have counter space, stove and utensils. You can use the same pots and spoons and other things as you do for cooking, just wipe the excess oil and wax off with paper towel and then wash as usual. Most of the ingredients are edible anyway.

If you spill essential oils wipe it up with a clean paper towel or cleaning rag, but don't throw it away; you can stuff it in a closet or drawer to make it smell good. Try not to get it on your hands. Unless you are allergic to plants of any kind it shouldn't be a problem, but it is better to be safe.

Equipment you may need:

Stainless steel double boiler
Or a crock-pot
Measuring spoons
Measuring cups, those little dosage cups on cough syrup are good for measuring too
Containers: amber bottles (with orifice reducer and lid or with an eyedropper lid), jars tins, small Ziploc disposable containers are good for body butters.
Stainless steel spoons
Paper towel
Old newspaper
Stainless steel or glass mixing bowl
Grater
Mixing bowl
Eyedropper
Bamboo Shish ka bob skewer – used to clean funnels and eyedroppers
Cotton balls – twist a bit of cotton around the tip of the skewer for cleaning
Funnels

Ingredients you may need:
The essential oils
Lavender hydrosol
Sea salt
Epson salt
Olive oil, or any other carrier oil, grape seed, jojoba, etc
Vitamin E oil
Shea butter
Bee's wax
Cocoa butter
Honey
Glycerin
Baking soda
Liquid body/hand soap
Citric acid

Basic Procedures:

Start with a clean area. Read the recipe to see what equipment and ingredients you will need and gather them all together. Then just follow the directions. Most of the ingredients in body butters and lip balms simply need to be melted on low heat. You do not want your ingredients to get too hot because that will break down some of the delicate chemical compounds of the oils you are using. Don't rush it; bee's wax will take some time to melt. (Microwaves don't heat things evenly) Remove the butters and wax from the heat source before you add essential oils. Then just pour your recipe into the containers and wait for it to cool and harden. While the pots and pans are still warm, wipe them and the other things that are waxy with paper towel or newspaper. The more you can wipe off the easier it will be to wash.

Design Your Own Fragrance

If you are designing your own fragrance blend and have no healing purpose in mind, you can follow all the suggestions, rules and tips for combining essential oils but what it all boils down to is weather or not you like it! Pick one main essential oil; place it on the table with the lid directly behind it (so you don't mix-up the lids). Then choose two or three more and place them on the table. Pick up your main choice and one other then waft them under your nose together, holding the secondary oil a slightly further from your nose. (To "waft" essential oils hold the bottle at least six to twelve inches from your face and wave them back and forth. If you put it directly under you nose it will be too strong.) Now hold the third choice in the hand with the secondary oil. Waft them under you nose. What do you think? Do you want to add another one or take one away? The choice is yours.

Lip Balm
The basic formula:
• ¼ cup (2oz) vegetable or nut oil
• ¼ to ½ ounce bee's wax (Bee's wax makes it firm, if you want the lip balm to be soft use less if you want it to be firm, which means it will stay longer on your lips, use more wax)
• 1 teaspoon honey or glycerin
• No more than 15 drops of essential oil

1. Heat the oil and beeswax in a double boiler on low heat until the beeswax has melted.
2. Remove from heat and whip with an electric beater until creamy (whipping is optional).
3. Add the honey or glycerin and approximately 5 drops of essential oil; whip some more. Add more essential oil if you want. By this time it should be cool enough to test on your lips to see if you want more essential oils.

4. Pour into your containers, when they are cool put the lids on.

If you want to add color you can add a small chunk of lipstick to the melting pot, just keep in mind that lipstick is NOT "all natural".

Suggested Essential Oil:

#1 Peppermint

Just peppermint oil, add just a few drops at a time, you don't want to get it too strong.

#2 Healing Lip Balm

One capsule of vitamin E oil

3 drops lavender oil

2 drops tea tree oil

1 drop rosemary oil

This recipe may not taste wonderful but it will heal cold sores and chapped lips wonderfully!

#3 Citrus Flavor

Use with honey – 2 or 3 drops of lemon, orange or bergamot essential oils. Not recommended for sunny weather.

#4 Hot and Fruity

1 drop of cinnamon oil

4 or 5 drops of orange, and/or lemon

Should feel gently warm and tingly, don't get it too strong,

#5 Lemon and peppermint

2 or 3 drops of peppermint oil

4 or 5 drops of lemon oil

Bath Salts Basic Recipe

3 cups of Epsom Salt or sea salt or a combination

1 cup of baking soda

Mix well and store in an air tight container. You can add essential oils when you first mix it up or you can scoop out a cup of salt then add your choice of essential oils as you need it. Add any essential oil you would like, mix well and let it sit at least one hour. For every cup of bath salt add 10 drops more or less of essential oil.

For fizzy bath salts
> 1 cup of bath salts
> 1 tablespoon citric acid

#1 Spicy Woodsy Smell (Mentally clarifying and may help you feel fortified, or more confident, also these oils are good for overly oily skin, or dry skin.)
To one cup of mixed bath salt add:
> 3 drops Cedarwood
> 2 drops Frankincense
> 1 drops Orange

#2 Relaxing and Healing (Recommended for minor injuries. You can use half a cup of mixed bath salt in a foot bath if you have an injury on your foot)
To one cup of mixed bath salt add:
> 6 drops lavender
> 3 drops tea tree

#3 Bedtime Bath (Soak in this bath for as long as you can without actually nodding off with your face in the water!)
> To one cup of mixed bath salt add:
> 3 parts lavender
> 3 parts chamomile
> 2 part orange

#4 Cold and Flu Season (For when you start to feel like you might be coming down with something)
> To one cup of mixed bath salt add:
> 4 drops lavender
> 2 drops tea tree
> 2 drops rosemary
> 2 drops eucalyptus

Salt Scrub or Skin Polish
> 1 cup sea salt
> 1 cup carrier oil
> 1 cup liquid soap

Mix well and add essential oils of your choice. This will need to be stirred every time you use it, the salt will settle to the bottom. Scrubbing stimulates your skin and improves circulation anyway so this blend will be a real eye opener, but don't get it in your eyes!

Essential Oil Suggestions:
You can use the same suggestions as for the bath salts.

#1 Wake-Up Scrub
     5 drops peppermint
     3 drops Cedarwood
     2 drops rosemary

#2 Glowing Skin Scrub (for sensitive, acne prone skin)
     5 drops bergamot
     3 drops chamomile
     3 drops lavender

Basic Lotion Bars
     2 oz. cocoa butter
     2 oz. beeswax
     2 oz. shea butter
     2 oz. any carrier oil

Melt all together in a double boiler on low heat, remove from heat to add essential oils, and then pour into a container. The container should be one from which you can easily pop out the lotion bar. The little disposable Ziploc containers with the blue lids work the best. If you want the bar to be less firm, use less wax. Being less firm means that more will melt onto your skin.

Essential Oils
Add a total of 10 to 20 drops of essential oils (or more if you want a strong fragrance)
For extra dry skin use: chamomile, geranium, lavender and a few drops of Niaouli or tea tree.
For sensitive or irritated skin use: chamomile and lavender
For a manly fragrance use: Frankincense, Cedarwood, orange and a touch of rosemary

You can use any of the essential oil combinations mentioned above or come up with your own combination. The cocoa butter and the shea butter have a strong fragrance (which isn't nearly as strong when it is cooled) so you may want to add more essential oils. Add just a few drops at a time, stir it in and sniff it to see if you like it.

Miscellaneous Recipes
Sunburn Spray
     To one spray bottle of lavender hydrosol add 15 drops of lavender oil. Shake well before spraying on sunburn.

First Aid Ointment
     1 oz. cocoa butter
     1/2 oz. beeswax
     1 oz. shea butter
     1 oz. olive oil

10 drops lavender
10 drops tea tree
5 drops rosemary

Melt all together in a double boiler on low heat, remove from heat to add essential oils, and then pour into a container. This is for bug bites cuts, scrapes, rashes, chapped lips, chapped skin, pimples, etc.

Bug Repellent
1 15ml amber glass bottle with an orifice reducer
10ml olive oil
20 drops citronella
10 drops eucalyptus
10 drops tea tree
10 drops Cedarwood

Add the olive oil to the bottle first, then the essential oils, put on the lid tightly. (The orifice reducer comes in the lid, when you screw the lid on tightly it is forced into the neck of the bottle and will stay there when you open it.) Shake well. This will help keep the bugs away and it is a good treatment for bug bites.

Study Aid
Simply add a few drops to a cotton ball and stick it in the air vent, or fold a piece of paper into a fan and drop the oil directly onto it, occasionally fan you face while you study. Studies show that if you use certain essential oils while you study for a test and when you take the test your scores will be improved.

Use peppermint and Cedarwood with lemon, lime and/or rosemary.

For Cellulite
Cellulite is one of the harder types of fats to dissolve in the body. Cellulite is an accumulation of old fat cell clusters that solidify and harden as the surrounding tissue loses its elasticity. Essential oils such as tangerine and grapefruit may help digest fat cells. Cypress enhances circulation to enhance the elimination of fatty deposits. Suggested Essential Oils: Rosemary, grapefruit, lemon, cypress, tangerine, lemongrass, Cedarwood

Recipe for Massage Oil:
9 drops lemon
9 drops cypress
2 oz of jojoba oil
Massage oils into the skin at least once daily and before exercising. Cellulite is slow to dissolve so target areas should be worked for a month or more in conjunction with weight training and a weight loss program.

Recipe for Bath
> 5 drops grapefruit
> 3 drops orange
> 3 drops cypress
> 3 drops lemon
> 2 tablespoons of honey

Mix the oils in the honey the dissolve in warm bath water.

PMS Recipes for Teens
Use these oil blends as massage oil or as perfume and dab on behind the ears. Also you can add the essential oils only to distilled water in a spritz bottle and use as an air freshener.
Add to ½ cup carrier oil:
For "Weepy" Times
> 5 drops orange oil
> 5 drops geranium oil
> 10 drops Clary-sage oil

For Angry Times
> 10 drops palmarosa
> 10 drops geranium
> 10 drops bergamot

For Irritable Times
> 5 drops of Chamomile
> 10 drops of Clary-sage
> 10 drops of bergamot
> 5 drops of geranium

For Colds and Sinus Trouble

Steam Inhalation Drop essential oils into a bowl of steaming water. Lean over the bowl and drape a towel over your head and bowl to hold in the steam. Close your eyes and breathe deeply until the water cools.

For Sinus
> 4 drops rosemary
> 2 drops thyme
> 3 drops of peppermint

For Colds and Flu
> 5 drops tea tree
> 1 drop eucalyptus
> 1 drop peppermint

For a Chest Rub
Mix in your palm:
    About a teaspoon of the first aid ointment
    1 drop eucalyptus
    1 drop peppermint

For a runny nose simply take a couple big sniffs of peppermint.

Bonus Bath and Body Recipe Collection

Here is a collection of bath and body recipes to try. Some of these recipes call for dried herbs.

A Sleep Inducing Bath

4 tb Dried chamomile
3 tb Dried lemon balm
2 tb Dried passionflower
1 tb Dried valerian

If you're feeling agitated at bedtime, the right herbal combination can help you drift right off into the REM stage. Put the dried herbs in a tea strainer, or tie it up in a square of muslin fabric, and drop it into the bath water. If you want to add essential oils mix a few drops of oil in a portion of bath gel before adding it to the water.

Note: Make bags out of muslin or cheesecloth. Decorate with trims and notions. Add ribbons so that the bags can hang from the faucet into the bath water. Fill bags with herbal bath mixtures.

Bath Salts #2

1/2 c Epsom salt
1/2 c Baking soda
1/2 c Borax
2 dr Food coloring
30 dr essential oil
Mix together and put in a pretty bottle.

Scented Bath Bombs
Number of Applications: 6
1 1/2 cups baking soda
1/2 cup citric acid
2 drops lavender essential oil
2 drops orange essential oil
2 drops bergamot essential oil
1/2 teaspoon sweet almond oil
2 drops food coloring -- your choice of color
-Combine all ingredients.
-Press into muffin tin or mold of your choice.
-Release from mold.
-Wrap in colored plastic wrap and tie with a ribbon.

NOTES : Fizzes when dropped in water.

Tangerine Dream Bath Salts
Chamomile-- 2 drops
Lavender--7 drops
Tangerine--9 drops
Sea Salt--3 tbsp
Baking Soda-- 2 tbsp
Borax--1 tbsp
Add sea salt, baking soda, borax and oils to jar. Gently shake to mix, mix well. Add to tub of running water.

Scented Bath Crystals
Number Of Applications : 4
1 cup Epsom salts
10 drops essential oil -- your choice of scent
1 drop food coloring -- your choice of color
-Mix all ingredients well.
-Store in bottle or bag.
NOTES : This makes a wonderful gift when poured in a decorative glass bottle. When selecting an oil for scent, read warnings about use. Some oils are not intended to have direct contact with skin.

Milk Bath

Basic Milk Bath
3 cups powdered milk
1/4 cup oatmeal
1/4 cup dried orris root (has a soft violet scent)
1/3 cup almond meal
1 capsule vitamin E (break open into dry ingredients)
1/3 cup cornstarch

This recipe makes enough for a few baths. Combine ingredients make sure it's completely mixed. Store in a container with a tight fitting lid. When you are ready to add it to your bath, scoop the desired amount of the mixture and tie securely in a muslin bag or even a facecloth will do, then add a few drops of your choice of essential oils. Tie to the faucet allowing the warm water to run over the bag.

* To make almond meal: Using a blender, grind up blanched or slivered almonds to a powdered consistency.

Milk and Honey Bath
Your skin will feel luxurious when you use this recipe. Milk baths are very skin softening, something that is wonderful at this time of year! Once you make this recipe, use it right away.

4 tablespoons honey; 1 quart boiling water; 6 tablespoons dried milk powder.

1. Place the honey in a bowl and add the boiling water. Stir until the honey has dissolved. Leave to cool.

2. Place the milk powder in a bowl and gradually mix in the honey water.

3. Add the milk mixture to a warm bath, swishing it about so the milk powder dissolves completely.

4. **Lock the bathroom, light some candles. Relax**!!

Meadow Milk Bath
Powdered Milk, finely sifted--4 oz
Citric Acid--2 oz
Corn starch--2 oz
Vitamin E Oil--One 400 IU Capsule (or Grapefruit Seed Oil--30 drops)
Jasmine--60 drops

Blend the powdered milk and corn starch, then sift. Mix vitamin E (or grapefruit seed oil) and Jasmine in Citric Acid. Make sure oils are thoroughly blended in the Citric Acid. Combine the Citric Acid blend with milk/corn starch blend.
Use 3 tablespoons per bath.

Lavender Getaway Bath
For a soothing winter bath, put 2 tablespoons of lavender buds (Lavendula angustifolia) and 2 tablespoons of finely ground oatmeal into a small muslin bag or a piece of cloth. Secure tightly with a string or a piece of ribbon so that it hangs under the faucet of your bathtub. Once the bath is full, try rubbing the bundle gently over your skin. Both the lavender and the oatmeal will work to soothe dry skin and calm frazzled nerves as well.

Bubble Bath

Basic Bubble Bath Recipe
Use only 100% pure soap flakes.
Almond Oil--2 cups
Distilled Water--2 cups
Soap Flakes (or grated soap)--1 cup
Witch Hazel--2 Tbsp
Boil the spring water and melt the soap in it. In another container, mix the witch hazel and almond oil together and shake well. (If possible, do this in a blender.) Then slowly add the soap mixture to the witch hazel and oil blend and again, shake or blend well. These amounts will make a large quantity of basic bubble bath mixture to which you can add the essential oils of your choice as and when required. For each 2 tablespoons of base bubble bath, use 15 drops of essential oil and mix well. Use 1-2 teaspoons of the final product in each bath.

Lavender Dreams Bubble Bath
Ingredients:
1 quart water
1 bar castile soap (grated)
3 ounces glycerin
15 drops lavender essential oil
5 drops chamomile essential oil
5 drops of orange essential oil
Directions:
Mix all ingredients together. Store in a container with a tight fitting lid. Pour in running water.

Tropical Dream Bubble Bath
Ingredients:
3 drops bergamot essential oil
2 drop jasmine fragrant or essential oil
1 ounce glycerin
1 ounce coconut oil
1 bar castile soap (grated)
1 quart water
Directions:
Mix all ingredients together. Store in a container with a tight fitting lid. Pour in running water.

Body Oil

Special Toxin Eliminator Bath
Massage the cellulite areas while they are under the water.
Place in the bath:
Epsom salts--2 handfuls
Rock salt--1 handful
Add 8 drops of this blend:
Basil--8 drops
Grapefruit--14 drops
Juniper--6 drops
Lemon--12 drops
Oregano--6 drops
Blend together.

Rich Body Oil
Sunflower Oil--4 oz
Hazelnut Nut Oil--1 tsp
Macadamia Nut Oil--1 tsp
Evening of Primrose Oil--1 tsp
Vitamin E Oil--20 drops
Mix and store in tightly covered bottle. Refrigerate for longer shelf life.

Pre-bath Oil
Base
Grapeseed Oil--2 Tbsp
Carrot Tissue--10 drops
Evening Primrose--10 drops
Jojoba--20 drops
Toning Oil
Black Pepper--4 drops
Ginger--3 drops
Lemongrass--6 drops
Use 5 drops Toning Oil in 1 teaspoon Base. Massage all over body before getting into the bath or shower. Use soap on only the body parts that really need cleaning so you don't wash off all the oil.

Anti-sorrow Bath Oil
Sweet Almond Oil--1 ounce
Marjoram--10 drops
Clary Sage--5 drops
Cypress or Rosemary--5 drops
Hyssop--1 drop
Melissa or Lemon--1 drop

Body Power

Aromatic Sachet Powder
4 Parts dried crushed Sweet Marjoram
2 Parts dried thyme
2 Parts dried crushed basil
1 Part caraway seeds
1 Part dried lemon peel
1 Part grated nutmeg

Baby Powder
1 c Arrowroot
1 c dried chamomile
In a blender, grind the chamomile to a fine powder. Rub it between your fingers to be sure there is no grit. Add the arrowroot and blend together. This is a great powder for diaper rash. This is also useful for adults with athlete's foot, heat rash, or other skin problems promoted by unventilated, moist conditions.

SIMPLE BATH POWDER
1/2 cup cornstarch
1/2 cup rice flour
4 drops essential oil
Place cornstarch and rice flour into blender. Add essential oil and mix well. Pour into a clean container.

Liquid Soap

Tangerine Body Wash
Coriander--7 drops
Grapefruit--10 drops
Lavender--7 drops
Tangerine--40 drops
Unscented Shower Gel--4 oz (aloe gel or mild liquid soap may be substituted, with varying results.)

Easy Liquid Soap
Take your favorite castile soap and grate it up until you have 1 *firmly* packed cup. Then add 3 c. almost boiling water. Stir with a whisk until it is thoroughly mixed (no lumps). When it has cooled, add your favorite essential oils. This makes a fairly large batch.

Simple Soap Recipe
Glycerin Soap and/or Castile Soap Flakes--1 lb
Essential Oil--1/4 oz (7.5 ml)
Purified Water--1 cup
Herbal Tea or Hydrosol--1/2 cup
Melt glycerin in double boiler, add herbal infusion or hydrosol. Let cool slightly...it needs to be pourable. Add essential oil. Stir well. Pour into molds or plastic-wrap lined box. Let harden, cut into bars. Smooth rough spots with knife.

Liquid Hand Soap #2
1 bar hand soap (any type), grated
1 cup boiling water
1 T. honey
1 tsp. glycerin (available at drug stores)
Put grated soap and boiling water into a blender and whip. Add honey and glycerin and stir in blender. Let it cool for 15 minutes and whip again. Add cold water until the mixture reaches the six-cup mark. Whip again. Pour into a storage container, and let cool for one hour with lid off. Shake before using.

Body Scrubs

Body Buffer
¼ cup Jojoba Oil
1/4 cup Liquid Soap
1/2 cup Sea Salt, Very Fine
10 drops Essential Oils, for circulation use tangerine, peppermint and bergamot
Combine all ingredients in a small bowl and mix thoroughly. Pour into a flip top bottle.

Field and Sea Body Scrub
3 tbsp Kelp Powder
3 tbsp Oatmeal
3 tbsp Orange Peel, grated
3 tbsp Sea Salt
3 tbsp Sunflower Seeds, ground
3 drops Grapefruit essential oil
Sweet Almond Oil
Save Sweet Almond Oil for later. Mix all dried ingredients and Grapefruit essential oil in a jar. Keep jar tightly closed until use. Blend with almond oil to a desirable consistency just before using.

Perfume

These perfume recipes call for vodka, it is not as drying to your skin as rubbing alcohol, it is the only good use of vodka.

Orient Nights Perfume
Ingredients:
4 drops Australian sandalwood
4 drops musk
3 drops frankincense
2 teaspoons jojoba oil
Directions:
Mix all the ingredients together, shake well. Then allow the perfume to settle for at least 12 hours. Store in a cool dry area.

Whispering Rain Perfume
Ingredients:
2 cups distilled water
3 tablespoons vodka
5 drops sandalwood essential oil
10 drops bergamot essential oil
10 drops cassia essential oil
Directions:
Mix all the ingredients together, shake well. Then allow the perfume to settle for at least 12 hours. Store in a cool dry area.

Falling Stars Perfume
Ingredients:
2 cups distilled water
3 tablespoons vodka
5 drops lavender essential oil
10 drops chamomile essential oil
10 drops valerian essential oil
Directions:
Mix all the ingredients together, shake well. Then allow the perfume to settle for at least 12 hours. Store in a cool dry area

Enchanted Perfume
Ingredients:
2 cups distilled water
3 tablespoons vodka
5 drops everlasting essential oil
10 drops peony essential oil
10 drops Australian sandalwood essential oil
Directions:
Mix all the ingredients together, shake well. Then allow the perfume to settle for at least 12 hours. Store in a cool dry area.

Solid Cologne
Ingredients:
3 parts carrier oil (sweet almond or Jojoba)
2 parts beeswax
1 Essential Oil
Melt the beeswax in a double boiler on low heat; add the carrier oil, then the essential oil. You might want to let the mixture cool a bit before adding the essential oil, so it doesn't dissipate from the heat. Pour into the tins and let cool completely before capping.